Lara Takes Charge

by Rocky Lang
and Sally Huss

(for kids with diabetes, their friends and siblings)

Lara Takes Charge
Written by Rocky Lang and Sally Huss
Illustrated by Sally Huss

Second edition

Published by:
Cable Publishing
14090 E Keinenen Rd
Brule, WI 54820

This is a work of fiction. Any resemblance to actual people, living or dead, is purely coincidental.

ISBN: 978-1-934980-05-7
Library of Congress #2004105698

To order additional copies of this book, please visit us at:
www.cablepublishing.com
nan@cablepublishing.com

 Printed in the United States of America

To Kevin and Mary and all at C.H.L.A.
and to Nikki, Lara and Erica for their courage.

ROCKY LANG

For my friend Billy.

SALLY HUSS

My name is Lara
and I am a normal kid.

I can do everything other kids can do.

I can run.

I can swim.

I can dance.

I can play.

I can think.

I can do anything I want,
    as long as Mommy or Daddy
    says it is okay, of course.

But there is one thing I <u>have</u> to do that most kids don't.

That is, I watch my blood sugar.
I have diabetes.

This means that a part of my body,
my pancreas, that is supposed to
control my blood sugar,
does not work very well.

So, I have to take insulin to keep
my blood sugar in a safe range.

I have a special meter to check
my blood sugar.

I have a special pump to give my body the insulin it needs.

I wear it all the time. I keep it in my pocket or wear it on my belt.

Sometimes Mommy or Daddy pushes
the buttons and sometimes I do.

Pushing the buttons makes the insulin
go into my body after I eat.

I eat good food with lots of fruits and vegetables, just like everyone else.

I eat dessert like ice cream, cookies or cake, just like everyone else.

Sometimes I get frustrated and mad, but everybody gets frustrated and mad sometimes.

Sometimes having diabetes
is not easy.

But because I take care of myself, I will
always be able to do <u>anything</u> I want.

Yes, I am normal as normal can be.
I love being me.

Talking Points

How do you get diabetes?
> You get diabetes when the part of your pancreas that produces insulin stops working.

What is insulin?
> Insulin is a hormone that allows sugar to go to the cells so that you have energy.

Can I catch diabetes (from you)?
> Diabetes is not contagious in any way.

Where is the pancreas in your body?
> It is behind the stomach and in front of your spine. It looks like a tadpole.

What happens if your blood sugar is out of range?
> When blood sugars go high or low, people feel different symptoms such as tired, or cranky or confused.

Does it hurt to test your blood sugar with the special meter / wear the pump?
> Sometimes it can hurt a little.

Is there anything I can do to help my friend with diabetes?
> The best thing to do to help your friend, is to treat them like everyone else.